from SEA TO SHINING SEA

ILLINOIS

By Dennis Brindell Fradin

CONSULTANT

Robert L. Hillerich, Ph. D., Consultant, Pinellas County Schools, Florida;
Visiting Professor, University of South Florida

CHILDRENS PRESS®
CHICAGO

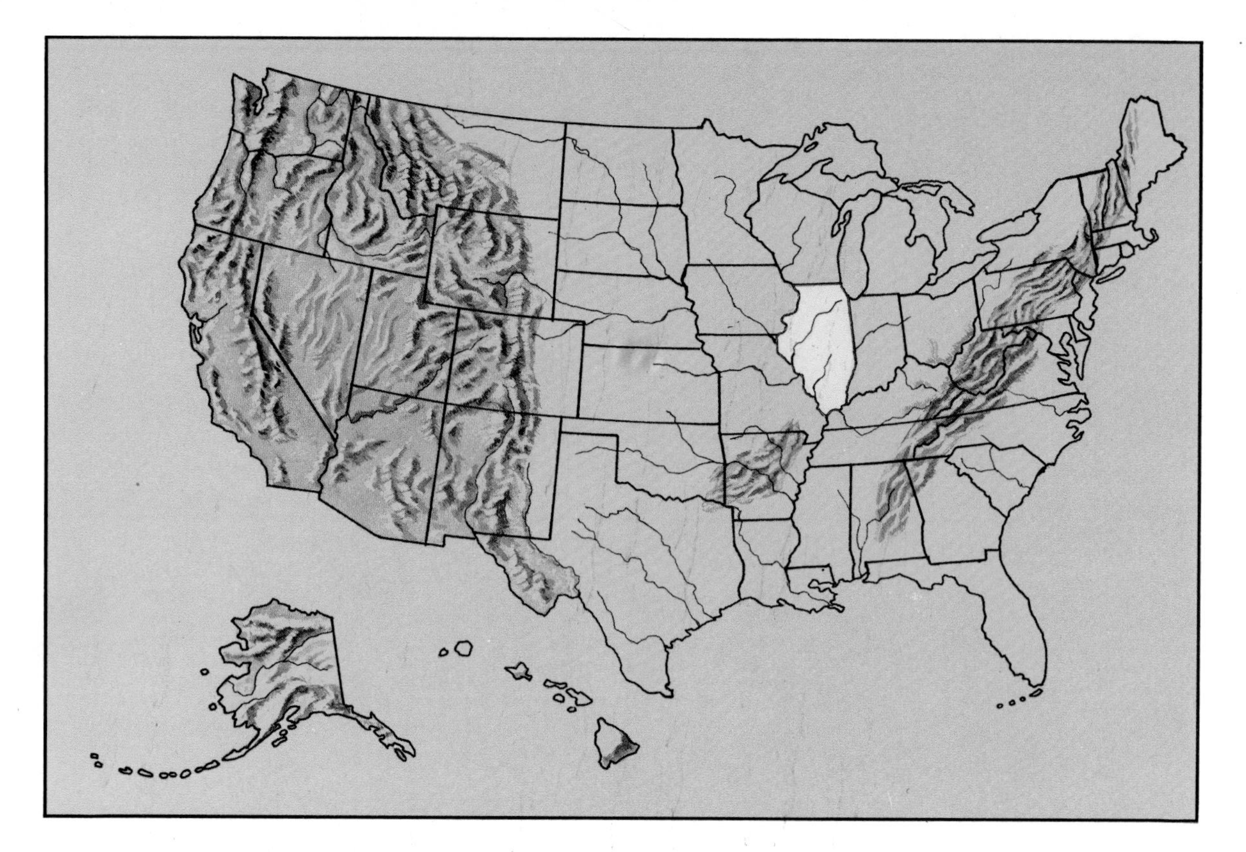

Illinois is one of the twelve states in the region called the Midwest. The other Midwest states are Michigan, Wisconsin, Indiana, Iowa, Ohio, Minnesota, Missouri, Nebraska, North Dakota, South Dakota, and Kansas.

For my dear son, Anthony Derrick Fradin

For his help, the author thanks David Blanchette of the Illinois Historic Preservation Agency.

Project Editor: Joan Downing
Design Director: Karen Kohn
Research Assistant: Judith Bloom Fradin
Typesetting: Graphic Connections, Inc.
Engraving: Liberty Photoengraving

SECOND PRINTING, 1992.

Printed in the United States of America.
2 3 4 5 6 7 8 9 10 R 00 99 98 97 96 95 94 93 92

Library of Congress Cataloging-in-Publication Data

Fradin, Dennis B.
From sea to shining sea. Illinois / by Dennis Brindell Fradin.
p. cm.
Includes index.
Summary: An introduction to the history, geography, important people, and interesting sites of Illinois.
ISBN 0-516-03813-3
1. Illinois—Juvenile literature. [1. Illinois.] I. Title.
F541.3.F68 1991 91-13510
977.3—dc20 CIP
AC

Chicago Cubs baseball fans at Wrigley Field

Table of Contents

Introducing the Land of Lincoln

Illinois is an average-sized state near the middle of the United States. Some states are known for making products. Others are known for farming. Illinois is a leader in both manufacturing and farming.

Chicago is the largest city in Illinois. The Chicago area is one of the greatest manufacturing centers in the country. Yet small towns and farms make up most of the state.

From the big city of Chicago to the smallest villages, most Illinoisans agree on one thing: Abraham Lincoln was the state's greatest person. Illinois' main nickname is the "Land of Lincoln." Illinois is also called the "Prairie State" because much of it is flat grassland.

The land of Lincoln has many other claims to fame. Where did the atomic age begin? Where do the Cubs play baseball and the Bears play football? What was the birthplace of President Ronald Reagan and author Ernest Hemingway? In what state is the world's tallest building located? As you will see, the answer to all these questions is: Illinois!

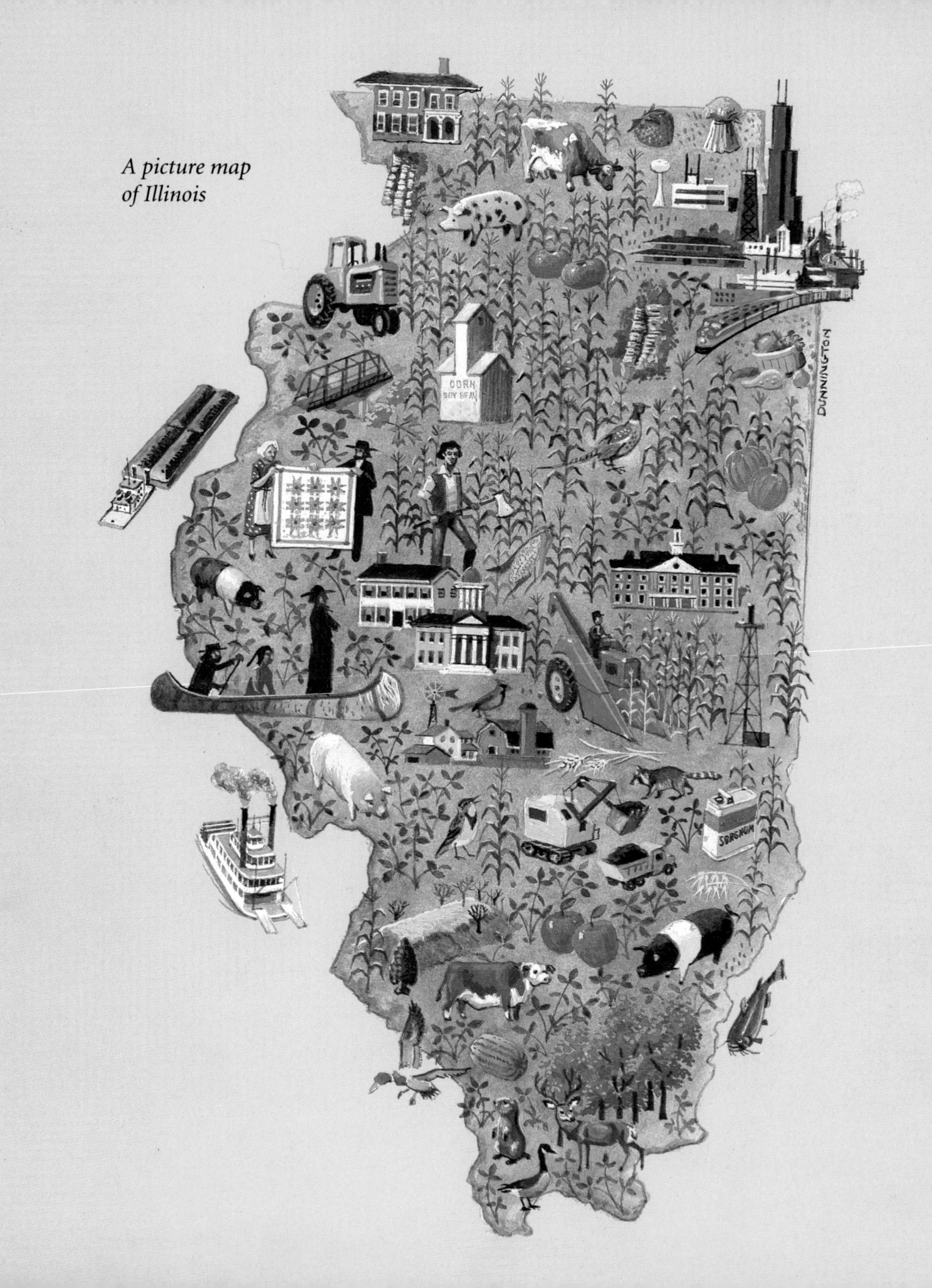

A picture map of Illinois

Flat Lands and Fertile Soil

Flat Lands and Fertile Soil

Illinois is shaped much like a key. It has been called the "Tall State" because of its shape. Illinois' tallest north-south distance is 385 miles. Its widest east-west distance is only 218 miles. The state's northern and southern tips are very far apart. They can even have very different weather on the same day. For example, it may be freezing in Chicago on a January day while southern Illinois is enjoying springlike weather.

Illinois is in the part of the country called the Midwest. Four of the eleven other midwestern states touch Illlinois. Wisconsin is to the north. Indiana is to the east. Iowa is to the west. Missouri borders the west and a small part of the south. Kentucky, a southern state, is south and southeast of Illinois.

Topography

Some major bodies of water lie along Illinois' borders. Lake Michigan splashes against northeast Illinois. It is the largest lake wholly inside the United States. The Mississippi River winds down

The Mississippi River is about 2,350 miles long.

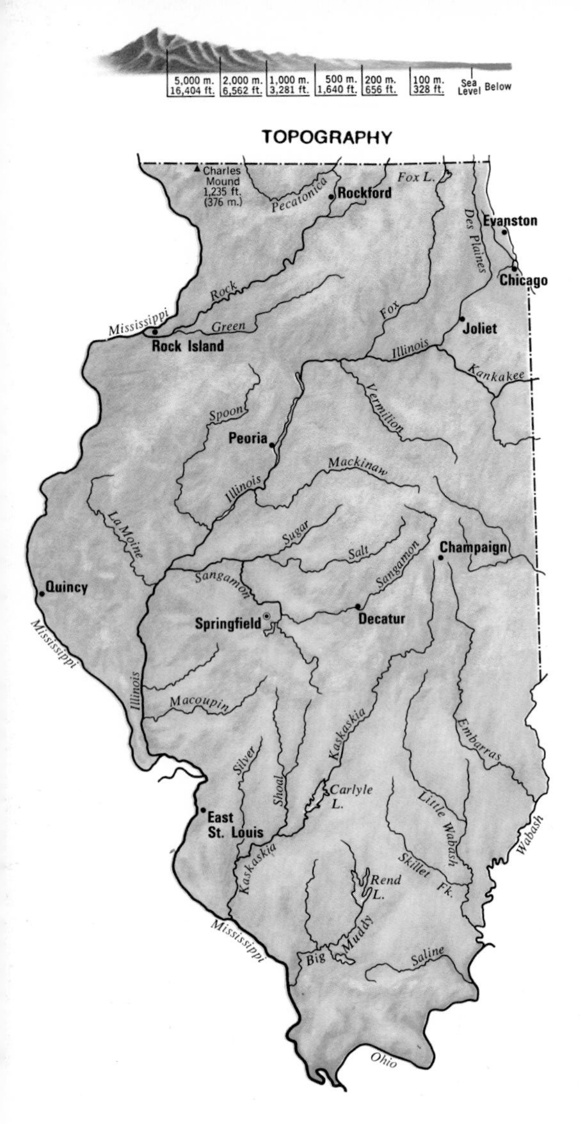

The fertile soil of Illinois makes it a great farming state.

Illinois' western edge. It is the nation's longest river. The Ohio River begins in Pennsylvania. It ends by flowing into the Mississippi River at Cairo, Illinois. The Wabash River winds down part of the Illinois-Indiana border. Rivers inside Illinois include the Illinois, Rock, Sangamon, Embarras, and Kaskaskia.

Illinois has no mountains. Parts of the state are hilly, but most of it is rather flat. The highest point

Left: The Mississippi River at Mississippi Palisades State Park
Right: Wildcat Canyon, in Starved Rock State Park

in Illinois is Charles Mound, near the state's northwest corner. Charles Mound is only 1,235 feet above sea level. Sears Tower, in Chicago, is more than 200 feet taller than that! Although it has no mountains, Illinois does have plenty of fertile soil. In fact, some of the richest soil on earth can be found in the Land of Lincoln. Its fertile soil is why Illinois is such a great farming state.

From Ancient Times Until Today

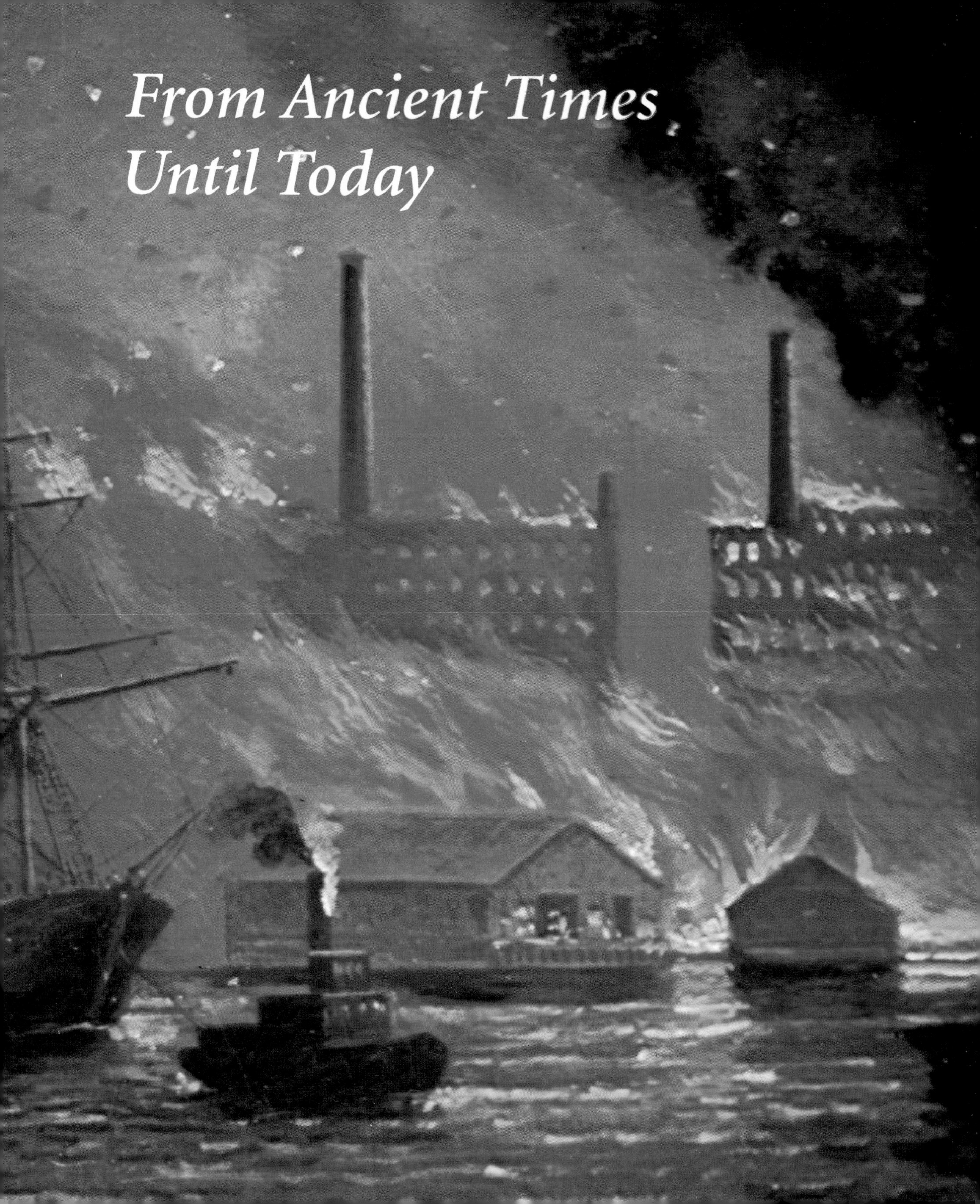

From Ancient Times Until Today

Many millions of years ago, Illinois was covered by shallow seas. Fish teeth and other sea fossils have been found in many places that are now dry land. The water helped create two treasures for Illinois. Over the ages, plants and animals that had lived in the water turned into coal and oil.

About two million years ago, the climate turned cold. The Ice Age began. Huge sheets of ice called glaciers covered about 90 percent of Illinois. Like giant bulldozers, the glaciers flattened the hills of Illinois. They also carried rocks and other material into the area. Over time, this material turned into the state's rich soil. The small areas untouched by the glaciers are now the hilliest regions in Illinois.

Illinois' highest point, Charles Mound, is in a region that the glaciers did not reach.

Prehistoric Indians first reached Illinois at least ten thousand years ago. Those early Indians hunted mastodons and other animals for food. Over time, they began farming. Several thousand years ago, the ancient Indians began building dirt mounds in much of America. More than ten thousand mounds were built in Illinois. Most of the mounds were burial places. Other mounds were platforms for

Mastodons, which looked like large, hairy elephants, died out long ago.

buildings. Monk's Mound, in southwest Illinois, once supported a large temple.

This is an artist's concept of what Monk's Mound once looked like. Monk's Mound is the largest Indian mound in North America. It is 100 feet (about ten stories) tall.

Early Illinois Indians

The ancient Indians may have been the ancestors of some of Illinois' later tribes. Six Illinois tribes united to help each other. They were the Cahokia, Kaskaskia, Michigamea, Moingwena, Peoria, and Tamaroa. The six tribes called themselves the Illini, meaning "the People." Illinois was named for the Illini. Other tribes in Illinois included the Winnebago, Chippewa, Sauk, Kickapoo, Ottawa, Potawatomi, Miami, Shawnee, and Fox.

The Indians were fierce in war. Yet in daily life, they were kind and gentle.

The Kickapoos (left) were among the Indians who lived in Illinois when the first white settlers arrived.

Modern-day actors reenact parts of the historic Marquette and Jolliet voyage of exploration.

French Rule

In the early 1600s, French explorers and fur traders began traveling south from Canada. One expedition set out in May 1673 to explore the Mississippi River. Explorer and fur trader Louis Jolliet was the leader. Jacques Marquette, a priest who knew Indian languages, went with Jolliet. Five other men went along.

On this trip, Marquette and Jolliet became the first known Europeans in Illinois. Canoeing down the Mississippi River, they reached northwest Illinois in June 1673. They went as far south as Arkansas. Then they turned around. On their return trip, they again passed through Illinois. This time, they traveled on the Illinois River. That route took them through the heart of Illinois. They became the first known Europeans to reach the site of what is now Chicago.

French explorer La Salle built a fort near present-day Peoria in 1680. In 1699, French priests founded Cahokia southwest Illinois. Kaskaskia was founded in 1703.

In 1717, Illinois became part of French Louisiana. But France never gained a strong hold on Illinois. To settle Illinois, families who would farm and put down roots were needed.

The fort built by La Salle in 1680 was called Fort Crèvecoeur (Fort Heartbreak). La Salle's full name was René-Robert Cavelier, Sieur de La Salle.

English Rule

The English were the main settlers of the country that became the United States. By 1733, England ruled thirteen American colonies. England wanted French Canada and the huge Louisiana region held by France. The French had their eyes on England's thirteen colonies. Between 1754 and 1763, England and France fought a war over North America. England won and took over nearly all French land in North America, including Illinois.

It was called the French and Indian War because many Indians helped France.

In the spring of 1775, the Americans began fighting the Revolutionary War against England.

The Americans wanted to free themselves from England and create their own country, the United States. Nearly all of the fighting took place in the East. But several major events occurred in Illinois.

In 1778, the Americans sent George Rogers Clark to capture English outposts in and near Illinois. Clark and his men took Kaskaskia and Cahokia from the English in the summer of 1778. That helped America win the Revolutionary War in 1783. A new flag now flew over Illinois: the Stars and Stripes of the United States.

Illinois had flown the French flag for about ninety years and the English flag for about twenty years.

The Road to Statehood

For a short time, Illinois was part of Virginia. In 1787, it became part of the Northwest Territory. In 1800, Illinois became part of the Indiana Territory. Finally, in 1809, the Illinois Territory was created.

Meanwhile, American settlers were moving to Illinois. Most came from southern states. By 1810, about twelve thousand settlers lived in Illinois. The Indians knew that one day the settlers might take all their lands. Between 1812 and 1815, the United States fought England in the War of 1812. The Indians sided with the English. In July 1814, in a battle near present-day Rock Island, Sauk Chief

Black Hawk defeated the Americans. But a much more famous battle took place in Chicago.

Chicago had been settled in the 1770s. Its first settler was Jean Baptiste Point du Sable, a black fur trader. The United States had built Fort Dearborn in Chicago in 1803. About fifty-five soldiers were in the fort early in the War of 1812. In the summer of 1812, American officials ordered Fort Dearborn abandoned. Everyone in Chicago was to move 150 miles away to Fort Wayne, Indiana.

On the morning of August 15, 1812, about a hundred soldiers and settlers left Fort Dearborn. Before they had gone even two miles, hundreds of Potawatomi Indians attacked. The Indians killed about half the travelers. They captured most of the rest and burned Fort Dearborn. Chicago was abandoned for the next four years after this Fort Dearborn Massacre.

Chief Black Hawk (above) fought the Americans during the War of 1812. Twenty years later, he was to fight the settlers in the Black Hawk War.

This is the way Fort Dearborn looked before being burned by the Potawatomis during the 1812 massacre. Several survivors of the Fort Dearborn Massacre helped rebuild Chicago in 1816.

Kaskaskia was washed away by Mississippi River floods in 1844 and 1881. A new town named Kaskaskia was later built nearby.

Illinois became the twenty-first state on December 3, 1818. Shadrach Bond was the first state governor. Kaskaskia was the first state capital. Vandalia became the capital in 1820.

The Young State

Illinois grew quickly in its first years as a state. The population quadrupled to about 160,000 between 1818 and 1830.

One newcomer to Illinois in 1830 was twenty-one-year-old Abraham Lincoln. That year, Lincoln moved with his family from Indiana. The Lincolns settled near Decatur. Lincoln helped his father build a log cabin and plant the crops. The next year, Lincoln moved to New Salem, where he worked as a store clerk. He tried to make up for his lack of schooling by reading all he could.

Abraham Lincoln became part owner of this New Salem store in 1832.

As newcomers arrived, they built new towns in Illinois. In 1819, Springfield was settled. In 1839, it became the capital. The southern third of Illinois was nicknamed Egypt by the pioneers. They thought it looked like the African country of Egypt. In the early 1800s, a town was settled at the southern tip of the state. It was named Cairo for the city of Cairo, Egypt.

The Indians were losing their lands to the settlers, as they had feared. In the early 1830s, the federal government forced many Indians to move west from Illinois into Iowa. Chief Black Hawk and a few hundred Sauk Indians made one last stand in Illinois. Many fights between Indians and settlers took place during the Black Hawk War of 1832. But the settlers were too strong for the Indians. In the end, the Sauks were almost wiped out and Black Hawk was captured. By 1840, only a few hundred Indians were left in Illinois.

The religious group known as the Mormons was begun in 1830 by Joseph Smith in New York State. For a few years, the Mormons moved from place to place. In the late 1830s, Joseph Smith and a few thousand other Mormons moved to Illinois. They founded Nauvoo. Their neighbors were jealous of

Nauvoo (below) was founded by the Mormons in the late 1830s. The Mormon Church is officially called the Church of Jesus Christ of Latter-day Saints.

the Mormons' success. Joseph Smith and his brother Hyrum were thrown in jail near Nauvoo. On June 27, 1844, a mob broke into the jail. They shot Joseph and Hyrum Smith to death. A short time later, the Mormons left Nauvoo and traveled to Utah.

Meanwhile, Chicago was changing from a small town into a giant city. From 1840 to 1860, Chicago's population grew from forty-five hundred to one hundred thousand.

By 1860, Chicago was by far the largest city in Illinois.

Chicago was midway between the western farms, ranches, and mines and the big eastern cities. Ships could reach Chicago from Lake Michigan or from the new Illinois-Michigan Canal. Finished in 1848, the canal linked the city with the Mississippi River system. By 1856, Chicago was the world's leading railroad center. Cattle, wheat, lumber, copper, and iron went to Chicago by train, boat, and wagon. Chicagoans used some of these goods to build their city. They sold the rest to other parts of the nation.

The Civil War

By the 1850s, Americans were arguing over slavery. In Illinois and the rest of the North, slavery was

Abraham Lincoln (left) and Stephen A. Douglas (right) debated the slavery issue during the 1858 campaign for the United States Senate. Lincoln once said that anyone who didn't think slavery was so bad should try it.

outlawed. But in the South, black slaves were forced to work on farms and large plantations. Most white southerners did not want to end slavery.

In 1858, Abraham Lincoln ran against Stephen A. Douglas for the United States Senate. The two men traveled around Illinois arguing about slavery. These talks are called the Lincoln-Douglas Debates. Lincoln called slavery "evil." Douglas was more accepting of slavery. Although Douglas won the election, Lincoln won great fame.

In 1860, the Republican party chose Lincoln to run for president. He won and became the sixteenth president of the United States. White southerners feared that President Lincoln would free their slaves. Eleven southern states left the Union. They formed

These Civil War pictures show Captain Peter Casey of the Irish Legion, 90th Illinois Regiment (left) and two unidentified "comrades at arms."

their own country. They called it the Confederate States of America, or the Confederacy.

Lincoln felt that the South had no right to leave the country. Most northerners agreed. The Civil War between the Union (the North) and the Confederacy (the South) began on April 12, 1861. Illinois sent about 260,000 troops to fight the Confederates. About 35,000 Illinois men died in the war.

John Wilkes Booth shot Lincoln. Booth was a southerner who blamed Lincoln for the South's defeat.

The Union finally defeated the Confederacy on April 9, 1865. As soon as the war ended, President Lincoln began planning to rebuild the South. He didn't get to do that. On April 14, 1865, Lincoln was shot. He died the next morning. During the

Civil War, Lincoln had taken steps to end slavery throughout America. For this, and for keeping the North and South together in one nation, he is remembered as perhaps our greatest president.

THE CHICAGO FIRE

A few years after the Civil War, disaster struck Chicago. On October 8, 1871, a fire broke out in Kate O'Leary's barn. Most Chicago buildings were made of wood. The weather had been dry. It was windy that day. Soon the fire was racing through Chicago. The Great Chicago Fire burned for thirty-one hours. At least three hundred people died. Nearly twenty thousand buildings burned. One hundred thousand people were left homeless.

The Great Chicago Fire, which broke out on October 8, 1871, left much of the city in ruins.

Architect Louis Sullivan designed Chicago's Carson Pirie Scott building.

"CHICAGO SHALL RISE AGAIN," said a Chicago newspaper. It did. Great architects such as Louis Sullivan and Daniel Burnham planned a new Chicago. Much of the new city was built with steel and concrete—materials that resist fire. One new structure was the ten-story Home Insurance Building. Completed in 1885, it was the world's first modern skyscraper.

INDUSTRY

Illinois was changing around the time of the Chicago Fire. In pioneer days, nearly everyone in Illinois had farmed. Starting in the mid-1800s, manufacturing also became important to the state. New inventions helped make this happen.

In 1837, Grand Detour resident John Deere invented a steel plow. It broke the prairie soil better than earlier plows did. Deere founded a plow-making firm in Moline in 1847. Cyrus McCormick of Virginia had invented a reaper in 1831. These machines could harvest grain much faster than farmers working by hand. In 1847, McCormick moved to Chicago and began making his reapers there. In 1875, Gustavus Swift began what became the famous Swift & Company meat firm in Chicago.

Aaron Montgomery Ward moved to Chicago in 1866. He began the country's first large-scale mail-order business in 1872. Richard Sears and Alvah Roebuck also thought Chicago would be a good place for a mail-order business. In 1893, they founded Sears, Roebuck and Company. By the 1890s, Illinois was third in the nation in manufacturing.

In the late 1800s and early 1900s, people came from all over the world to work in Illinois factories. Thousands of black families also moved to Illinois from the South.

Left: Sausage makers at a Chicago meat-packing plant
Right: A family from the South arriving in Chicago in 1910

Prohibition, Depression, and War

In 1920, Prohibition went into effect in the United States. This law banned the making and selling of liquor. But people drank liquor anyway. Often they bought it from gangsters. The gangsters fought over who would sell liquor.

The most famous Chicago gangster was Al Capone. "Big Al" ordered many murders. From 1926 to 1930, there were about two hundred gangland killings in Chicago. The city became more peaceful in the early 1930s. Al Capone was jailed and the United States ended the law against liquor.

By then, the Great Depression (1929-1939) had begun. During this period of great hardship, many businesses closed. People lost their jobs and their homes. By 1933, 1.5 million Illinoisans were out of work.

At times during the Great Depression, Illinois factories were using only half of their usual work force.

The biggest war the world has known helped pull the country out of the depression. This was World War II (1939-1945). The United States entered the war in 1941. About a million men and twenty thousand women from Illinois served the country. Factories in Chicago, Peoria, and other cities made airplane engines and tanks. Illinois farmers helped win the war by feeding the troops.

About twenty thousand Illinoisans died in World War II.

During World War II, an event that changed the course of history took place in Illinois. The location was a University of Chicago lab. The date was December 2, 1942. On that day, Enrico Fermi and other scientists set off the first man-made nuclear chain reaction. This marked the birth of the atomic age. The atomic bomb has been one result of this. A peaceful result was the building of nuclear power plants.

Recent Events

Two atomic research centers were founded in Illinois. Argonne National Laboratory was founded

Enrico Fermi (left) headed a group of a scientists who set off the first man-made nuclear chain reaction. This sculpture on the University of Chicago campus (below) is a reminder of the event.

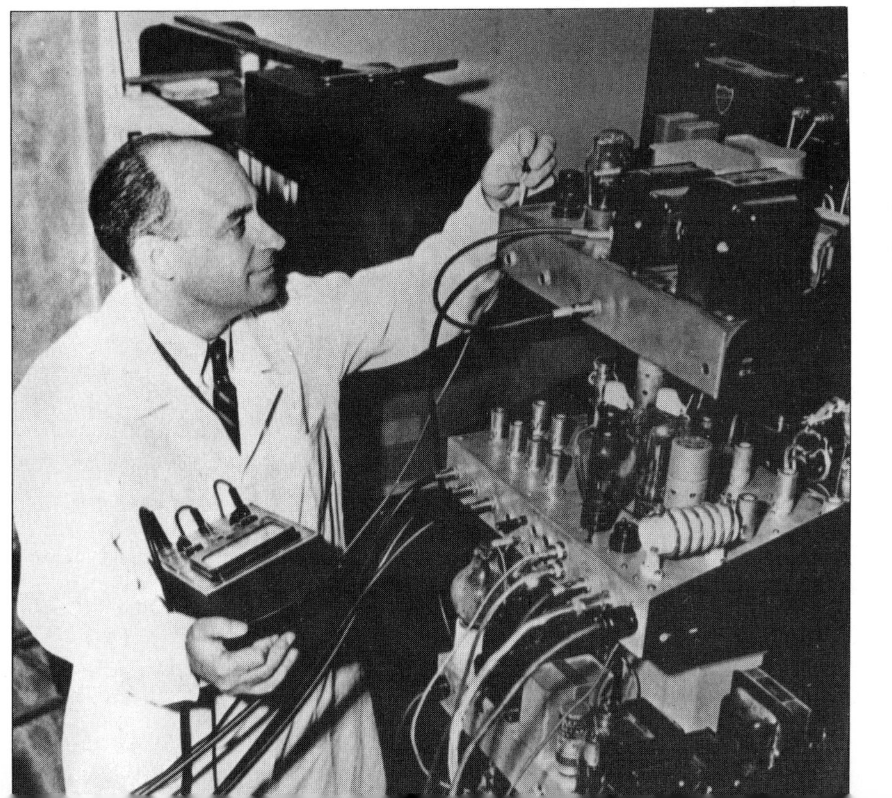

Fermilab was named for Enrico Fermi.

near Chicago in 1946. Fermilab opened in 1972, also near Chicago. Both are among the world's leading centers for research on the atom.

Droughts are long periods of little or no rain.

Since the end of World War II, two groups of Illinoisans have had rough times. The state's smaller farmers make up one group. High costs, low prices, and droughts have forced thousands of farmers into other lines of work. Between 1978 and the late 1980s, the number of Illinois farms dropped from 105,000 to 89,000.

The many poor people in Illinois cities make up the other group. Since about 1950, large numbers of richer people have moved from the cities to the suburbs. Many businesses have also left for the suburbs. Such cities as Chicago and East St. Louis, Illinois, have been left with numerous poor people. Many of them are black or members of other minorities. These people have trouble finding jobs. They often lack good housing. Their neighborhoods are plagued by drugs and crime. Their schools are usually of poor quality.

Illinoisans are now working to improve their schools. In 1989, Chicago began giving parents more control over their children's schools. People around the country are watching this new program. If it works in Chicago, it may work elsewhere.

Ronald Reagan is the only president of the United States who was born in Illinois.

In 1991, Illinois began a campaign to improve schools in every Illinois city and town. The state will watch the schools closely to make sure they are doing a better job of teaching children. A good education often leads to a good job, so better schools should help millions of Illinoisans in the future.

One small-town Illinoisan went very far in recent years. His name is Ronald Reagan, and he was born in Tampico in northwest Illinois. Reagan became a movie star. Later, he entered politics. In 1980, he was elected president of the United States. Ronald Reagan served as our fortieth president from 1981 until 1989.

Illinoisans and Their Work

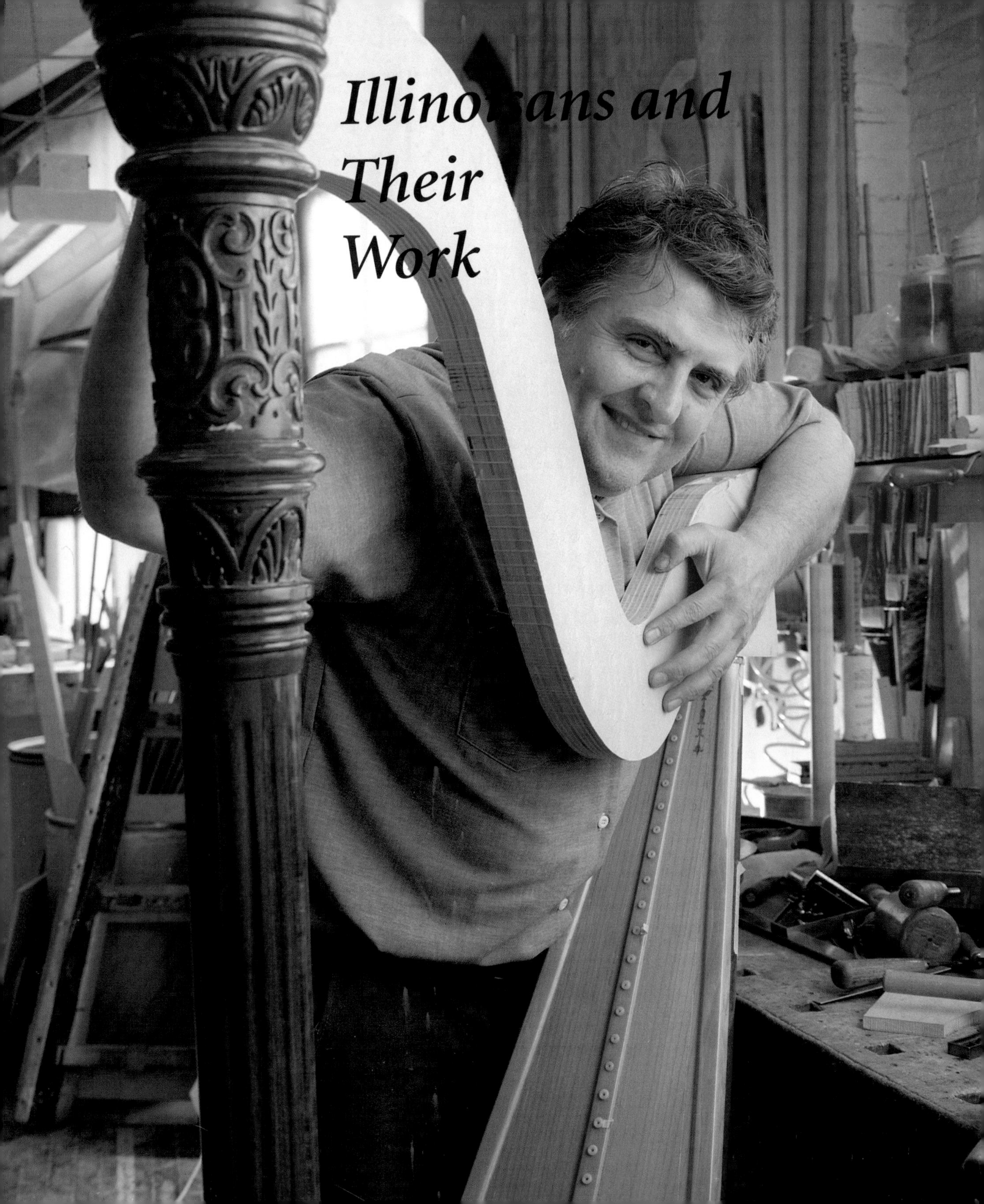

Illinoisans and Their Work

By 1990, 11.5 million people lived in Illinois. The only states with more people were California, New York, Texas, Florida, and Pennsylvania.

Illinois is made up of people of many national origins, many skin colors, and many religions. About 1.7 million Illinoisans are black. The state has nearly a million Hispanics (people of Spanish-speaking heritage). Nearly a third of a million Illinoisans are Asians. Illinois also has large numbers of people of Polish, German, Irish, Greek, Russian, Native American, and many other backgrounds.

Nearly one million Hispanic people live in Illinois. This girl is taking part in a Mexican Independence Day parade.

Making or selling products is the main kind of work in Illinois. The state is a leader in making tractors, bulldozers, and other kinds of machinery. Illinois is also a top steel-making state. Candy, cakes, corn syrup, breakfast cereal, butter, cheese, flour, and pet food are among the many foods that are packaged in Illinois. Other Illinois products include radios and television sets, cars, tires, and medicines. You are using one Illinois product this very second. This book was produced in Chicago, which is a big publishing center.

Farming also means a lot to Illinois. Corn is the state's leading farm product. Only Iowa grows more corn than the Land of Lincoln. Each year, Illinois produces about 1.5 billion bushels of corn. That comes to about 200 billion ears of corn. Strung end to end, the corn would reach for 20 million miles—nearly the distance from the planet Earth to the planet Venus! The corn has many uses. People and livestock eat it. Corn syrup is used to sweeten medicines. Corn is also used in many other products, from paper to fertilizer.

Illinoisans work at many different jobs, including farming (left) and directing television programs (right).

Soybeans are the state's second-leading farm product. Illinois usually leads the nation in growing

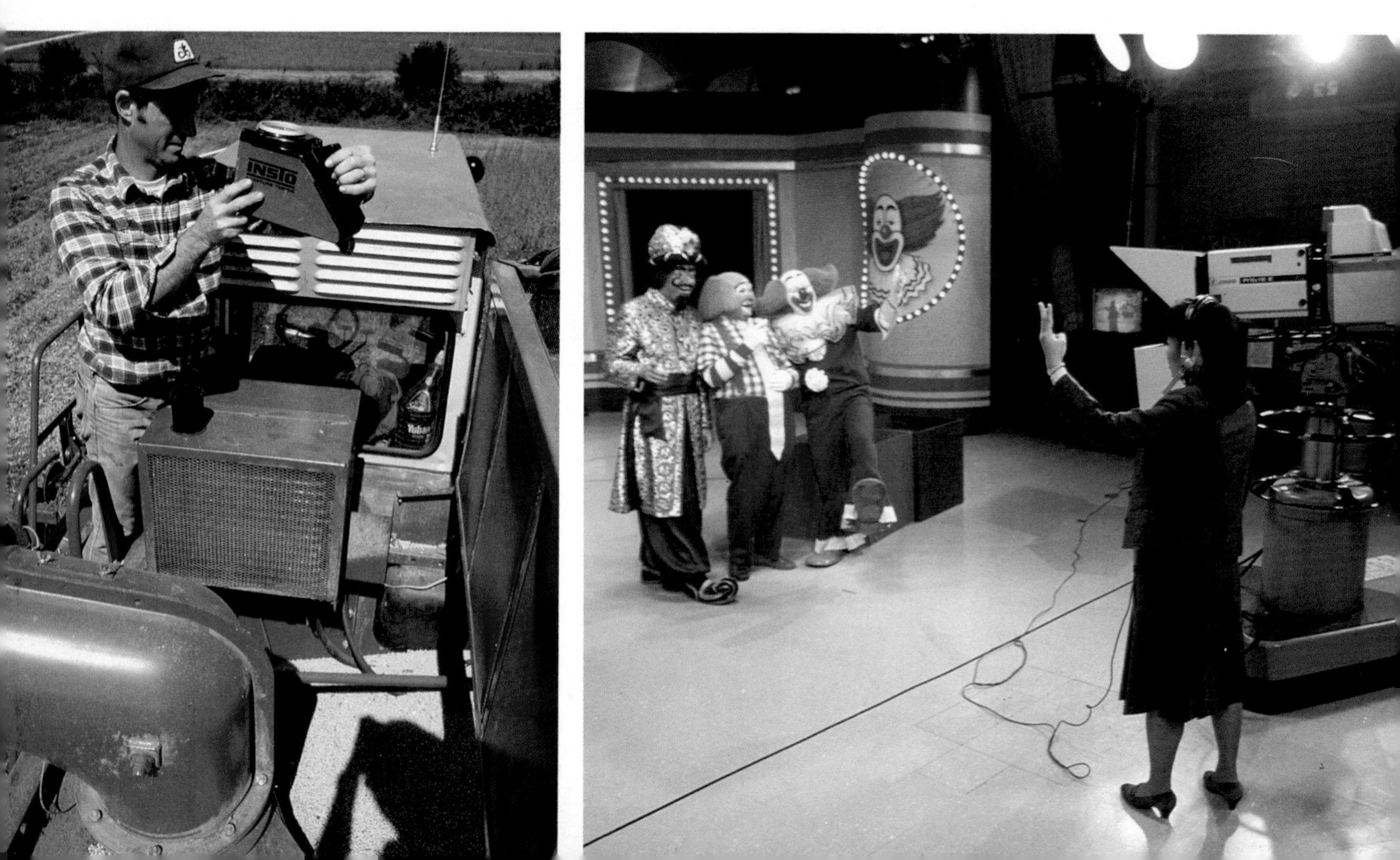

soybeans. The soybeans are used mainly as animal feed. Soybean foods for people include soy sauce, tofu, margarine, cooking oils, and salad dressings.

Wheat, hay, oats, and barley are other Illinois crops. Many Illinois farmers also raise livestock. Hogs, beef cattle, dairy cattle, and chickens are the main livestock animals.

A few thousand Illinoisans work at mining coal and oil. Illinois is one of the top five coal-mining states. It is one of the top fifteen oil-producing states. Illinoisans also work as teachers, bus drivers, doctors, lawyers, builders, telephone operators, government workers, and at many other jobs.

The travel industry (left) and newspaper publishing (right) employ many Illinois workers.

A Trip Through

the Land of Lincoln

A Trip Through the Land of Lincoln

Illinois is a wonderful state to visit. It has many historic sites. It has interesting cities and towns. And it has more beauty than most people realize. Chicago is a good place to start a trip through Illinois. The city lies on Lake Michigan in northeastern Illinois. Chicago is the nation's third-biggest city. Only New York City and Los Angeles have more people.

Chicago

Chicago's O'Hare Field is the world's busiest airport.

Chicago is nicknamed the "City of the Big Shoulders." Author Carl Sandburg coined the name in the early 1900s. The nickname fits, for Chicago is a big, strong city. Chicago is also called the "Windy City." It is often very windy in Chicago, but that's not why it got that nickname. A New York City writer coined the name in the late 1800s. He thought Chicagoans were "windy" because they bragged so much about their city.

Chicagoans still have plenty to brag about. The Windy City is the nation's top transportation center. Many railroads and highways go through Chicago.

Left: *This view from the Chicago River shows the 333 West Wacker Drive building (left), and Sears Tower (center).* Right: *Chicago's Wrigley Building*

And Chicago's O'Hare Field is the world's busiest airport.

Chicago is also one of the nation's top manufacturing centers. Thousands of products are made in and near Chicago. Among them are machines, metals, books, and many kinds of foods. In addition, Chicago is the banking center of the Midwest. Chicago's LaSalle Street is a famous banking area.

Chicago is famous for its skyscrapers. One of them, the Sears Tower, is the world's tallest building. The Sears Tower rises 110 stories above the Windy City.

Left: The Water Tower and the Hancock Building
Right: A beluga whale at the John G. Shedd Aquarium's new Oceanarium

Other Chicago landmarks include the Water Tower and Buckingham Fountain. The Water Tower survived the Chicago Fire. Buckingham Fountain is the world's biggest fountain with lights. Each summer, its spraying water and colored lights make a beautiful show.

Dating from 1930, the Adler Planetarium is the oldest planetarium in the United States.

Chicago has some of the world's best museums. At the Adler Planetarium, images of the stars and planets are shown on the ceiling. The Shedd Aquarium displays many kinds of fish and other sea animals. The Field Museum is known for its Egyptian mummies and dinosaur skeletons. The

Museum of Science and Industry is famous for its coal mine. Chicago's Art Institute has paintings by famous artists. Chicago also has a fine black-history museum, the Du Sable Museum of African American History.

Chicago is a big center for higher education. The University of Chicago is on the South Side. The University of Illinois at Chicago is on the West Side. De Paul and Loyola universities are also in the city.

Two major-league baseball teams play in Chicago. The Cubs play in Wrigley Field, which is known for its vines on the outfield wall. The White

Left: A waterfall in Lincoln Park Zoo's new bird house
Right: Wrigley Field

Chicago Bulls basketball star Michael "Air" Jordan led his team to the 1991 World Championship.

Sox play in new Comiskey Park, which opened in 1991. The Chicago Bulls, made popular by Michael Jordan, are the city's pro basketball team. The Bears are the city's famous pro football team. The Blackhawks are its pro hockey team.

Chicago is a city of neighborhoods. The city has neighborhoods where most people are of Polish background. Other areas are mostly Irish, Jewish, Chinese, Greek, or Italian. But black people are by far the largest minority in Chicago. Nearly half of all Chicagoans are black. About a fifth of the city's people are Hispanic.

Chicago has more than ten thousand black-owned firms. Many Chicago firms are owned by Hispanics. Yet huge numbers of Chicago's black and Hispanic people are very poor. Many of their neighborhoods suffer from crime and drugs. Improving life for its poor people is the greatest challenge facing Chicago.

Arlington Heights, Glenview, and Skokie are three other well-known Chicago suburbs.

Thousands of people who work in Chicago live in its nearby suburbs. Dozens of suburbs cluster near Chicago. Evanston, an old Chicago suburb, is the main home of Northwestern University. Oak Park is known for its many houses designed by Frank Lloyd Wright. Brookfield is home to the wonderful Brookfield Zoo. Wilmette has the famous

The dining room of the Frank Lloyd Wright Home and Studio in Oak Park

Baha'i Temple, a house of worship of the Baha'i religion.

NORTHERN ILLINOIS

Rockford is the state's second-biggest city. It is a manufacturing center. Auto parts are made there. Other Rockford products include machine tools, nuts and bolts, airplane parts, chewing gum, and men's socks.

Rockford has some interesting museums. The Time Museum has clocks dating back to the 1500s.

The Zitelman Scout Museum displays uniforms from the early days of the Boy Scouts and Girl Scouts. Visitors to the Erlander Home can learn about Rockford's early Swedish settlers.

The homes of two presidents are not too far from Rockford. West of Rockford in the northwest corner of the state is Galena. In 1860, Ulysses S. Grant (1822-1885) moved to Galena. Born in Ohio, Grant had served in the United States Army but had quit. He came to Galena to be a clerk in his father's leather store. Grant, his wife, and their four children rented a small home on High Street.

When the Civil War began, Grant rejoined the army. He rose to become one of President Lincoln's

Left: A farm in the northwest corner of Illinois near Galena
Right: The Ulysses S. Grant home in Galena

best generals. After helping the United States win the Civil War, Grant returned to Galena as a hero. Galena people gave him a large home, where he lived for a time. Then in 1868, Grant was elected the nation's eighteenth president. After eight years in office, he returned to his home in Galena.

The cottage on High Street where Grant lived while working for his father can still be seen. The house on Bouthillier Street given to him by the people of Galena can be toured.

Ronald Reagan was the only president born in Illinois. Reagan's hometown, Tampico, is southeast of Galena. On Tampico's Main Street is the apartment where Reagan was born in 1911. At that time, there was a restaurant-bakery beneath the apartment. When he was nine, Reagan moved with his family to nearby Dixon. At his home in Dixon, you can see the bedroom Ronald shared with his older brother.

Abraham Lincoln was born in Kentucky, but spent most of his life in Illinois. Ulysses S. Grant was born in Ohio.

Central Illinois

South of Dixon is Illinois' third-largest city, Peoria, which lies on the Illinois River. Peoria is the headquarters of Caterpillar Inc. This huge firm makes bulldozers and other heavy machinery. Other products made in the Peoria area include wire and trucking equipment.

The Wildlife Prairie Park is a highlight of Peoria. It has animals that are native to the state. Among them are deer, buffalo, elk, bobcats, bears, and eagles.

Illinois has more than seventy-five colleges and universities. Of the forty-nine other states, only New York, Pennsylvania, and California have more.

Southeast of Peoria are two major universities. Illinois State University is in Normal. The University of Illinois is at the twin cities of Champaign and Urbana.

Decatur, southwest of Champaign-Urbana, was laid out in 1829. When Abraham Lincoln and his family moved to Illinois in 1830, they first settled near Decatur. Their farm is now the Lincoln Trail Homestead State Memorial. The log cabin Lincoln helped his father make has been rebuilt.

Farmers ship corn and soybeans to Decatur. These crops are packaged in the city. In 1920, George Halas founded a pro football team in Decatur. It was called the Decatur Staleys. Halas moved the club to Chicago the next year. He soon changed its name to the Chicago Bears.

One of the most interesting places in Illinois is west of Decatur. It is called Lincoln's New Salem State Park. Abraham Lincoln moved to New Salem when he was twenty-two. During the six

Left: A cabin in Lincoln's New Salem State Park
Right: The Illinois State Capitol, in Springfield

years he lived there, Lincoln became a lawyer and entered politics. In 1837, he moved to Springfield. By the 1850s, New Salem was a ghost town. Finally, in the 1930s, the state of Illinois rebuilt New Salem to look as it did when Lincoln lived there.

Springfield is southeast of New Salem. It was made the state capital in 1839. Springfield has been the capital ever since. The capitol building has a big dome. When the legislators are meeting, visitors can watch them make laws for Illinois.

Before the capitol building went up, Illinois lawmakers met in the Old State Capitol. That building displays an original copy of a famous Lincoln speech: the Gettysburg Address. Other items that belonged to Lincoln are also on display.

Abraham Lincoln's Springfield home has been restored to look as it did in 1860.

The Lincolns' Springfield home is at the corner of Eighth and Jackson streets. Lincoln and his wife, Mary Todd Lincoln, lived in this house for seventeen years. They raised their four children there.

Abraham Lincoln left Springfield in early 1861 to become president. He never saw Springfield again. Lincoln was shot and killed in Washington, D. C., in April 1865. He was buried in Springfield. On his tomb are the famous words spoken by Secretary of War Edwin Stanton when Lincoln died: "Now he belongs to the ages." Lincoln's son Tad said some less-famous words at that sad time: "They killed my pa! They killed my pa!"

Southern Illinois

There are no big cities in southern Illinois. There are plenty of farms, though. Southern Illinois is a big wheat-growing area. It is also the state's main region for mining coal and oil.

Southern Illinois holds one tragic record. The area is often hit by tornadoes. On March 18, 1925, the deadliest tornado in history whirled across far southern Illinois. This mighty storm killed more than six hundred Illinoisans. It also killed about a hundred people in Missouri and Indiana.

Because it killed people in three states, the terrible storm is called the Tri-State Tornado.

The Shawnee Hills near the state's southern tip would be a good place to end an Illinois trip. This region has lovely hills and valleys. It has caves that can be explored. One of them is Cave-in-Rock on the Ohio River. It once was a pirates' hideout. The Shawnee Hills also have thick forests and beautiful lakes and rivers. Another highlight of the hills is the Garden of the Gods. The rocks there were carved into strange shapes by millions of years of water and wind.

People aren't the only ones who love southern Illinois. Birds such as great blue herons, quails, wild turkeys, and Canada geese can be seen in the region. Deer can be spotted in the woods. Other wild animals that live in Illinois include squirrels, raccoons, opossums, skunks, badgers, and coyotes.

The Shawnee National Forest, in southern Illinois

A Gallery of Famous Illinoisans

A Gallery of Famous Illinoisans

Abraham Lincoln, Ulysses S. Grant, and Ronald Reagan were very famous Illinoisans. Many other famous people have also lived in the Land of Lincoln.

Jean Baptiste Point du Sable (1745?-1818) was probably born in Haiti. He was part African and part French. Around 1770, du Sable settled where Peoria now stands. There he married an Indian woman. They had at least two children. Sometime in the 1770s, du Sable became Chicago's first settler. He built a cabin and trading post there. Du Sable grew rich in the fur trade. Other fur traders joined him and Chicago began to grow. In 1800, du Sable sold his Chicago holdings and moved away. He died in Missouri at about the age of seventy-three.

Du Sable and his wife had a son, Jean, and a daughter, Susanne.

Black Hawk (1767-1838) was born in a Sauk village on the Rock River near what is now Rock Island. When he was only twenty-one years old, Black Hawk became a Sauk chief. When the settlers were pushing his people out of Illinois, Black Hawk fought them during the War of 1812. Later, he fought them in the Black Hawk War of 1832. By then, he was sixty-five years old. Black Hawk died in Iowa when he was seventy-one.

Illinois has given birth to an amazing number of great authors. **Carl Sandburg** (1878-1967) was one of the best. Sandburg was born in Galesburg. As a young man, he traveled the country as a hobo. Later, he became a famous writer. He wrote *Abraham Lincoln: The Prairie Years* and other books about the sixteenth president. He also wrote many poems, including "Chicago."

Carl Sandburg wrote a poem called "Chicago" that gave the city one of its nicknames: "The City of the Big Shoulders."

Ernest Hemingway (1899-1961) was born in Oak Park. He fought in World War I and was badly wounded. Hemingway often wrote about war. Two of his best novels are *For Whom the Bell Tolls* and *The Old Man and the Sea.* Many people feel that Ernest Hemingway was the best American writer of the 1900s.

Ernest Hemingway was one of America's best writers.

Lorraine Hansberry (1930-1965) was born in Chicago. She became a playwright. Her first play was *A Raisin in the Sun.* It is about a black family that wants to escape from a poor Chicago neighborhood. The play won the New York Drama Critics Circle Award in 1959. Lorraine Hansberry was the first black writer to win this award. Hansberry didn't get to write much more, for she died when she was only thirty-four.

Jane Addams (left) founded a settlement house in Chicago in 1889. A settlement house is a place where neighborhood people can get help.

Jane Addams (1860-1935) was born in Cedarville. In 1889, she and her friend Ellen Starr founded Hull House in Chicago. It was one of the nation's first settlement houses. Jane Addams headed Hull House for forty-six years. She also helped get laws passed to protect Illinois' working children and women.

Jackie Joyner-Kersee is one of the best athletes to come from Illinois. She was born in East St. Louis in 1962. In 1988, she competed in the track and field events at the Olympic Games in South Korea. She won a gold medal for the long jump. She also won a gold medal in the heptathlon. That contest is made up of seven events. Jackie Joyner-Kersee has been called the "World's Greatest Woman Athlete."

Other famous Illinois athletes include former Chicago Bear running back **Walter Payton** and Chicago Bulls basketball star **Michael Jordan**.

Illinois was also the birthplace of a man who may have brought more joy to children than any other American in history. His name was **Walt Disney** (1901-1966) and he was born in Chicago. Disney moved to Missouri as a child but later returned to Chicago and studied art. Disney became a movie cartoonist. He created Mickey Mouse and Donald Duck. He also made full-length cartoon films, including *Snow White and the Seven Dwarfs, Fantasia,* and *Cinderella.* In 1955, he opened Disneyland, a famous amusement park in California.

Jackie Joyner-Kersee (left) and Walt Disney (right) were born in Illinois.

Harold Washington (1922-1987) was born in Chicago. He earned his law degree from Northwestern University in 1952. In 1964, Washington ran for the Illinois House of Representatives and won. For nearly twenty years, he served in the Illinois legislature and the United States House of Representatives. Then in 1983, he ran for mayor of Chicago. Harold Washington's warmth and concern for people won over voters of all colors. He won the election and became Chicago's first black mayor. "Harold," as Chicagoans called him, helped build better understanding among the city's different kinds of people. He also brought many women, blacks, and Hispanics into city government. Harold Washington died in office at the age of sixty-five.

Harold Washington was mayor of Chicago from 1983 to 1987.

The home of Abraham Lincoln and Ulysses S. Grant . . .

The birthplace of Ronald Reagan, Jane Addams, Chief Black Hawk, and Walt Disney . . .

The site of the country's biggest Indian mound and the Garden of the Gods . . .

The place where the atomic age began and where the Cubs and Bears play . . .

This is Illinois, the Land of Lincoln!

Did You Know?

Three Miss America winners came from Illinois. Lois Delaner, of Joliet, was the 1927 Miss America. Judith Anne Ford, of Belvidere, wore the crown in 1969. Marjorie Judith Vincent, of Oak Park, was Miss America for 1991.

The most lopsided championship game in National Football League history was played in 1940. The Chicago Bears beat the Washington Redskins 73-0!

One of Abraham Lincoln's nicknames was "Long Abe" because he was 6 feet, 4 inches tall.

The tallest known person who ever lived was Robert Pershing Wadlow (1918-1940), who was born in Alton. He was 8 feet, 11 inches tall—more than 2 1/2 feet taller than Abraham Lincoln.

In his early years, Ronald Reagan worked as a Chicago Cubs radio announcer.

Illinois has towns named Aroma Park, Coal City, Energy, Equality, Farmer City, and Industry.

Illinois also has towns named Blue Island, Grayville, Green Valley, Red Bud, and White Hall.

The original Ferris Wheel was built for the 1893 World's Columbian Exposition in Chicago. It was built by and named for George W. G. Ferris of Galesburg. The wheel was so huge that more than two thousand people could ride on it at once!

Big-league baseball's highest-scoring game ever was played in Wrigley Field on August 25, 1922. The Philadelphia Phillies scored twenty-three runs, but the Cubs won with twenty-six!

The deadliest fire in American history occurred on October 8, 1871. Although that was the day of the Chicago Fire, that famous fire is not the record holder. That same day, the Great Peshtigo Fire in and around Peshtigo, Wisconsin, killed about fifteen hundred people.

Each year, the United States and Canada have National Fire Prevention Week. It is held in October, during the anniversary of the Great Chicago Fire.

The world's largest post office building is in Chicago. Cars can drive through a tunnel that cuts right through this post office.

Pekin, Illinois, was named for Peking, China, by Ann Eliza Cromwell, an early settler there. Supposedly, she thought the town was exactly opposite Peking, China. (It's not.) We don't know what happened to the *g* at the end of Peking.

Softball was invented in 1887 by George Hancock in Chicago.

Illinois Information

Area: 56,345 square miles (twenty-fourth among the states in size)

Greatest Distance North to South: 385 miles

Greatest Distance East to West: 218 miles

Border States: Wisconsin to the north; Indiana to the east; Kentucky to the southeast and south; Missouri to the west and a small part of the south; Iowa to the west

Highest Point: 1,235 feet above sea level (Charles Mound near the state's northwest corner)

Lowest Point: 279 feet above sea level (in far southern Illinois along the Mississippi River)

Cardinal

Hottest Recorded Temperature: 117° F. (at East St. Louis, on July 14, 1954)

Coldest Recorded Temperature: -35° F. (at Mount Carroll, on January 22, 1930)

Statehood: The twenty-first state, on December 3, 1818

Origin of Name: Illinois was named for the Illini Indians

Capital: Springfield

Previous Capitals: Kaskaskia and Vandalia

Counties: 102

Violets

United States Senators: 2

United States Representatives: 20 (as of 1992)

State Senators: 59

State Representatives: 118

State Song: "Illinois," by Charles H. Chamberlain (words) and Archibald Johnston (melody)

State Motto: "State Sovereignty, National Union"

Nicknames: "Land of Lincoln," "Prairie State," "Tall State"

State Seal: Adopted in 1868

White oak tree

State Flag: Adopted in 1915

State Flower: Violet

State Bird: Cardinal

State Tree: White oak

State Animal: White-tailed deer

State Insect: Monarch butterfly

State Fish: Bluegill

Border Rivers: Mississippi, Ohio, Wabash

Some Rivers Inside Illinois: Illinois, Rock, Sangamon, Embarras, Kaskaskia, Spoon

Wildlife: Deer, foxes, raccoons, opossums, skunks, badgers, coyotes, squirrels, rabbits, ducks, geese, quail, wild turkeys, blue herons, many other kinds of birds, snapping turtles, painted turtles, other kinds of turtles, bass, catfish, perch, many other kinds of fish

Farm Products: Corn, soybeans, wheat, hay, oats, barley, apples, hogs, beef cattle, dairy cattle, chickens

Mining: Coal, oil, clay, sand and gravel, crushed stone

Manufactured Products: Tractors, bulldozers, and many other kinds of machinery, steel, many kinds of packaged foods, radios and television sets, cars, tires, medicine, books and other printed materials, nuts and bolts, tools, surgical equipment

Population: 11,466,000, sixth among the states (1990 U.S. Census Bureau figures)

Major Cities (1990 Census):

Chicago	2,783,726
Rockford	139,426
Peoria	113,504
Springfield	105,227
Aurora	99,581
Decatur	83,885

Monarch butterfly

White-tailed deer

Illinois History

During the Revolutionary War, George Rogers Clark and his men captured Kaskaskia and Cahokia from the English.

8000 B.C.—Prehistoric Indians live in Illinois

1673—Louis Jolliet and Father Jacques Marquette explore Illinois for France

1680—French explorer La Salle builds Fort Crèvecoeur (Fort Heartbreak) near present-day Peoria

1699—French priests found Cahokia

1703—Priests found Kaskaskia

1763—England wins the French and Indian War and takes a huge amount of land, including Illinois, from France

1778—George Rogers Clark and his men capture Kaskaskia and Cahokia from the English

1783—The United States wins the Revolutionary War

1787—Illinois becomes a part of the Northwest Territory

1800—Illinois becomes part of the Indiana Territory

1809—Illinois Territory is created

1812—Indians kill dozens of Chicagoans in the Fort Dearborn Massacre

1818—Illinois becomes the twenty-first state on December 3

1839—Springfield becomes the Illinois capital

1850—The population of Illinois reaches about 850,000

1858—Abraham Lincoln and Stephen A. Douglas conduct the Lincoln-Douglas Debates

1861—Abraham Lincoln becomes the sixteenth president of the United States

1861-65—About 260,000 Illinoisans fight for the North during the Civil War

1865—Abraham Lincoln is assassinated

1869—Ulysses S. Grant becomes the eighteenth president of the United States

1871—The Great Chicago Fire

1885—The world's first modern skyscraper is built in Chicago

1889—Jane Addams and Ellen Starr found Hull House

1900—The population of Illinois reaches nearly 5 million

1903—Fire in Chicago's Iroquois Theater kills more than six hundred people

1917-18—More than 350,000 Illinoisans help the United States and its allies win World War I

1929-39—During the Great Depression, many Illinoisans lose their homes, farms, and jobs

1941-45—About a million men and twenty thousand women from Illinois help the United States and its allies win World War II

1942—The atomic age is born at the University of Chicago

1946—Argonne National Laboratory is built near Chicago

1950—The population of Illinois reaches about 8,700,000

1968—Happy 150th birthday, state of Illinois!

1971—Illinois' current state constitution goes into effect

1972—Fermilab, an important center for atomic studies, opens near Chicago

1981—Ronald Reagan, born in Tampico, becomes the fortieth president of the United States

1990—Illinois' population reaches about 11.5 million

1991—James R. Thompson retires as governor of Illinois after serving for fourteen years

1992—Water from the Chicago River floods Chicago's entire underground tunnel system, causing about $1 billion in damage

Ronald Reagan's boyhood home in Dixon

MAP KEY

Place	Grid
Alton	E3
Argonne National Laboratory	B5
Arlington Heights	B5
Aroma Park	C5
Aurora	B4
Belvidere	A4
Blue Island	B5
Brookfield	B5
Cahokia	F3
Cairo	H4
Cave-in-Rock	G5
Cedarville	A3
Champaign	D4
Charles Mound	A3
Chicago	B5
Coal City	C4
Decatur	D4
Dixon	B3
East St. Louis	F3
Embarras River	E,F5
Energy	G4
Equality	G4
Evanston	B5
Farmer City	D4
Fermilab	B4
Galena	A3
Galesburg	C3
Garden of the Gods	G4
Glenview	B5
Grand Detour	B3
Grayville	F5
Green Valley	D3
Illinois River	C3
Illinois-Michigan Canal	B4
Industry	D2
Joliet	B5
Kaskaskia	G3
Kaskaskia River	E,F3,4
Lake Michigan	A,B5
Lincoln's New Salem State Park	D3
Mississippi River	A,B2,3;C,D,E2;F,G,H3
Moline	B3
Monk's Mound	F3
Mount Carroll	A3
Nauvoo	C2
New Salem	D2
Normal	C4
Oak Park	B5
Ohio River	G,H4,5
Pekin	C3
Peoria	C3
Red Bud	F3
Rock Island	B2
Rock River	B3
Rockford	A4
Sangamon River	D3
Shawnee Hills	G4
Skokie	B5
Spoon River	C3
Springfield	D3
Tampico	B3
Urbana	D5
Vandalia	E4
Wabash River	F5
White Hall	E3
Wilmette	B5

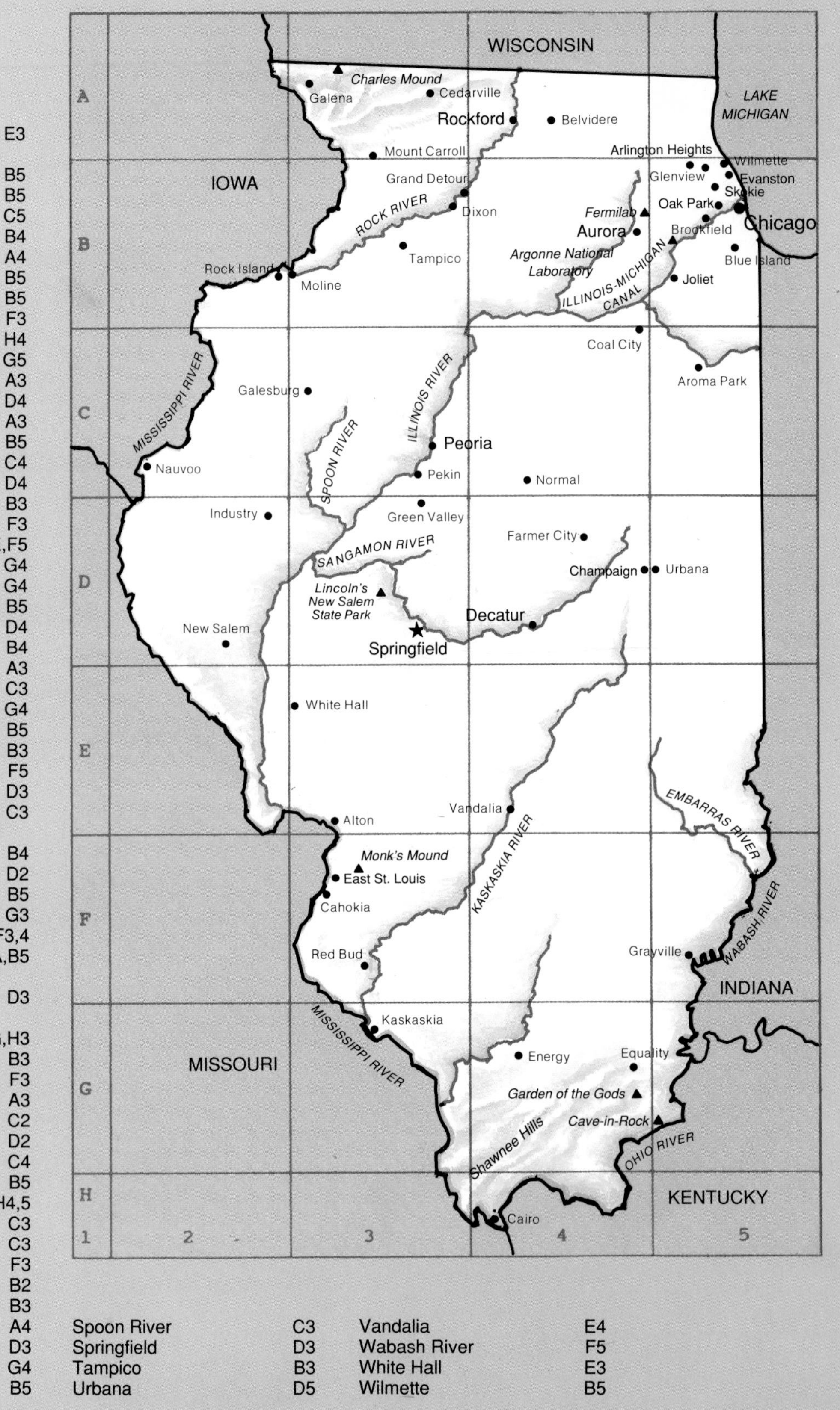

GLOSSARY

allies: Nations that unite to help each other for a common purpose

ancestor: A person from whom one is descended, such as a grandfather or a great-grandmother

ancient: Relating to those living at a time early in history

architects: Building planners

banned: Forbidden by law

capital: The city that is the seat of government

capitol: The building in which the government meets

coined: Made up, or invented

competed: Took part in a contest

current: Of the present time; the most recent

debates: Formal discussions

depression: A period of low business activity that leads to rising unemployment

disaster: A sudden event that causes much suffering, such as a flood, an earthquake, a tornado, or a fire

expedition: A journey of discovery

explorer: A person who travels in unknown lands to seek information

famous: Well known

fertile: Able to produce crops easily

firm: A company; a business

founded: Began; started; established

glacier: A large mass of ice that moves slowly down a slope or over a large area of land

invention: Something made, or created, for the first time

landmarks: Historic buildings, monuments, or sites

massacre: The act of cruelly killing a number of helpless people

minorities: Groups that differ in race, religion, or ethnic background from the larger part of a population

occurred: Happened

officially: Authorized, or legally approved, by the government

outposts: Frontier settlements

pioneer: One of the first to settle in a territory

plagued: Harmed; afflicted; damaged

prehistoric: Before written history

priest: A kind of minister or religious leader

quadrupled: Multiplied by four

research center: A place where investigation or experimentation is carried on

settlement house: A place where neighborhood people can get help

site: The place where something such as a town or a building has been built or will be built

skyscraper: A very tall building

suburbs: Towns or villages near large cities

tragic: Very sad or terrible

united: Joined

PICTURE ACKNOWLEDGMENTS

Front cover, © Mark Segal/**Tony Stone Worldwide/Chicago Ltd.**; 1, © Terry Donnelly/**Tom Stack & Associates**; 2, **Tom Dunnington**; 3, © Robert Frerck/**Odyssey Productions**; 5, **Tom Dunnington**; 6, **© Tony Stone Worldwide/Chicago Ltd.**; 8 (left), **courtesy of Hammond Incorporated, Maplewood, New Jersey**; 8 (right), © T. Dietrich/**H. Armstrong Roberts**; 9 (both pictures) © Terry Donnelly/**Tom Stack & Associates**; 10-11, **© SuperStock**; 13 (top), **Louisiana Office of Cultural Development**; 13 (bottom), © R. Flanagan/**Image Finders**; 14, © Robert Lightfoot III/**Nawrocki Stock Photo**; 15, **© Virginia R. Grimes**; 17 (top), **Chicago Historical Society** ICHi-08714; 17 (bottom), **Illinois State Historical Library**; 18, © John Patsch/**Journalism Services**; 19, **Historical Pictures Service, Chicago**; 21 (both pictures), **Library of Congress**; 22 (both pictures), **Chicago Historical Society** (left, ICHi-09740; right, ICHi-08059); 23 (left), **Historical Pictures Service, Chicago**; 23 (right), **Illinois State Historical Library**; 24, **© Cameramann International Ltd.**; 25 (both pictures), **Historical Pictures Service, Chicago**; 27 (left), **Historical Pictures Service, Chicago**; 27 (right), **© Cameramann International Ltd.**; 29, **Reagan Presidential Library**; 30, **© Eric Futran Photography**; 31, © Robert Frerck/**Odyssey Productions**; 32 (left), © Roy E. Roper/**H. Armstrong Roberts**; 32 (right), **© Cameramann International Ltd.**; 33 (both pictures), **© Cameramann International Ltd.**; 34-35, © Terry Donnelly/**Tom Stack & Associates**; 36, **© SuperStock**; 37 (left), **© SuperStock**; 37 (right), © Terry Donnelly/**Tom Stack & Associates**; 38 (left), © Terry Donnelly/**Tom Stack & Associates**; 38 (right), Edward Lines, Jr./**Baker & Assoc., Inc.**; 39 (left), **© James P. Rowan**; 39 (right) © S. Reed/**H. Armstrong Roberts**; 40, **Wide World Photos, Inc.**; 41, **photo by Judith Bromley, courtesy of the Frank Lloyd Wright Home and Studio Foundation**; 42 (left), © T. Dietrich/**H. Armstrong Roberts**; 42 (right), © Bill Crofton/**Journalism Services**; 45 (left), © Ken Dequaine/**Third Coast Stock Source**; 45 (right), © Bill Crofton/**Journalism Services**; 46, © John Patsch/**Journalism Services**; 47, © G. Ahrens/**H. Armstrong Roberts**; 48, **© Tom Dietrich**; 50 (top), **Illinois State Historical Library**; 50 (bottom), **Historical Pictures Service, Chicago**; 51, **Historical Pictures Service, Chicago**; 52 (both pictures), **AP/Wide World Photos**; 53, **Wide World Photos, Inc.**; 54 (left), **© 1990 Miss America Pageant/Photo by Kathleen A. Frank**; 54 (right), **Nawrocki Stock Photo**; 55 (left), **Chicago Historical Society**; 55 (right), **© Journalism Services**; 56 (top), **courtesy Flag Research Center, Winchester, Massachusetts, 01890**; 56 (middle), © Mark Reinholz/**Marilyn Gartman Agency**; 56 (bottom), © Rod Planck/**Dembinsky Photo Associates**; 57 (top), © Ruth Smith/**Root Resources**; 57 (middle), © Sharon Cummings/**Dembinsky Photo Associates**; 57 (bottom), © Skip Moody/**Dembinsky Photo Associates**; 58, **Historical Pictures Service, Chicago**; 59, © Tom Dietrich/**Tony Stone Worldwide/Chicago Ltd.**; 60, **Tom Dunnington**; back cover, © Gary Irving/**Tony Stone Worldwide/Chicago Ltd.**

INDEX

Page numbers in boldface type indicate illustrations.

About the Author

Dennis Fradin attended Northwestern University on a partial creative scholarship and graduated in 1967. He has published stories and articles in such places as *Ingenue, The Saturday Evening Post, Scholastic, Chicago, Oui,* and *National Humane Review.* His previous books include the Thirteen Colonies series and the Young People's Stories of Our States series for Childrens Press, and *Bad Luck Tony* for Prentice-Hall. In the True Book series, Dennis has written about astronomy, farming, comets, archaeology, movies, space colonies, the space lab, explorers, and pioneers. He is married and the father of three children.

DATE DUE

Metro Litho
Oak Forest, IL 60452

2/3/93	2.27.04 3B		
5M 12/8/95	3.5.04 3B		
12/11/96 3MM	3-10-04 3B		
1-22-99 5M	3-11-04 3B		
2-19-99 5M	4.2.04 3B		
2-17-00			
3-15-01 3M			
3-22-01 3M			
2/15/01 3M			
3M			
2.6.04 3B			
2.26.04 3B			